Small Firms' Attitudes to E-Business
Research Study 47
Mike Joseph, ORC International

The Law Society

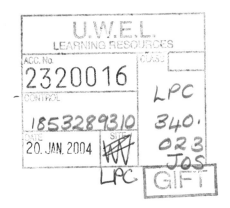

Acknowledgements

The author would like to thank Greg Barfoot and Doug Komiliades of ORC International for their assistance in the preparation of this report.

The Law Society

Contents

Foreword

This qualitative report complements the survey findings reported in *Solicitors' Involvement in E-business*. Together, these quantitative and qualitative studies sought to provide the Law Society with some assessment of small and medium-sized firms' readiness for e-business — that is, the use of information and communication technologies (ICT) both to improve and enhance existing working practices and business models within firms; and to give rise to new forms of products and services and new ways of dealing with other parties.

Two features of the survey results, in particular, were most striking. Although the overall profile for firms of this size was encouraging, in half of the firms there were fee earners who did not use the most basic of software. Second, almost without exception, uptake and use of PCs and internet technologies was lowest in sole practitioner firms and highest in firms with 5–10 partners. The survey also revealed that further development is required if firms are to be more fully engaged with e-business.

The prevailing vision of the impact of ICT on the legal market is that developments will move IT from data processing to true information management and that, in twenty years, the legal market will be segmented in three ways:

- 'traditional'— in which lawyers will serve clients in the familiar relationship;
- 'commoditised' — in which routine legal matters will be serviced by paralegals heavily supported by IT;
- the new 'latent legal market' — in which customers, who have been constrained by expense and access to legal material, will benefit from legal information services.

The government has accepted this vision and sees a role for ICT in reducing the payments made to solicitors. The Woolf Reforms sought to enable greater access to justice via ICT and instigated moves towards fees — in some areas at least — being based on value added for clients rather than on hourly rates for time spent. The expectation is that charges in some areas will fall due to use of improved in-house know-how and work product systems; the provision of online legal guidance systems; and legal information services provided at high volume and low cost.

The government's commitment to this notion is evidenced by its target of making all public services available online by 2005. The Land Registration Act 2002, for instance, authorises the Land Registrar to establish, run and regulate an electronic conveyancing system which will facilitate simultaneous completion and registration. The Court Service's Money Claims Online facility is up and running. Increasingly, other organisations with significant market power, such as banks, will also come to expect solicitors to conduct business electronically.

Change is upon the profession. It is evident from the comments made by some solicitors that the degree of change, and its long-term impact, may not be fully appreciated by many members of the profession. Solicitors, and firms, need to harness and embrace the commercial opportunities to develop online legal systems and to work with other professions to develop multi-disciplinary advice systems. As the report demonstrates, some entrepreneurial, pragmatic and adventurous firms are already revolutionising their organisations and ways of dealing with clients in a small number of areas.

The Law Society already provides services to help firms in this area. The Law Management Section (which has 1,800 member firms) provides information and guidance on a range of ICT matters affecting smaller practices and regularly runs seminars, conferences, exhibitions and features ICT articles in its quarterly magazine. The *Software Solutions Guide* aims to provide independent analysis about alternative practice management systems available in the legal-IT market place. Each year various books and publications on ICT are published by the Society.

A major purpose of this study was to provide information which would help the Law Society to identify other ways in which it can realistically support firms in this transition. Participants were asked for their views. Alongside some very helpful suggestions, some comments appeared to reveal a desire for the Law Society to provide specific answers, direct advice, or all embracing guides about ICT, geared towards particular needs. Just a few perspectives on firms allude to the difficulties involved in even attempting to do this. Sole practitioners are commonly identified as a distinct group with distinct needs but within that group there are many manifestations. Sole practitioner firms encompass a range from one-man bands (and people working part-time and from home) to firms with total employee numbers equalling or exceeding those of many firms with 5–10 partners. In all size-bands, different firms offer services in different legal areas, in different permutations and combinations of them, and using different methods — all requiring different management approaches. Increasing specialisation is another feature of the market and this might be approached by some firms in terms of specialist roles within the work of solicitors or by others in terms of particular legal areas — again, each approach requires a different ICT solution.

The solicitors' profession is too diverse in make-up, and provides too broad a range of advice and representational services for the Law Society to be able to provide specific, tailored advice about appropriate ICT uptake for every possibility. Overall, however, the findings presented in this report, and the many other helpful suggestions about what the Law Society can do to help, will make a very important contribution to the development of a strategy, over the coming year, to assist the profession in meeting the challenges of e-business.

Executive summary

About the research

The research described in this report was conducted in June 2003, amongst small to medium-sized private practice firms (defined as those with ten or fewer partners) in England and Wales.

The research forms the second, qualitative, phase of a two-stage project, following on from a quantitative telephone survey conducted between October and December 2002. The project as a whole was designed to aid the Law Society's Practice Development Team in the development of a strategic policy to support small and medium-sized firms in their use of information and communication technology (ICT) and e-business.

In this phase of the research, a total of 25 legal practices participated in eight discussion groups, each containing between two and five participants, conducted in London, Bristol, Birmingham and Manchester.

The ICT environment

The extent to which staff had access to and use PCs and the Internet appeared to be mainly a function of individual preference and experience. Partners and fee earners were often free to choose how much they used computers personally, rather than made to follow a strict policy.

Whilst there was some concern about misuse of the Internet, the benefits of the Internet were widely appreciated, especially as a resource for research and information gathering, and as a source for obtaining legal forms.

Opinions on e-conveyancing, however, were more divided. Whilst some recognised the benefits of speeding up the process, there was some concern that law firms had been insufficiently consulted on this development and were losing some control of the conveyancing process, with a consequent potential threat to the quality of work.

Email was seen as a useful additional mode of communication, complementary to other communication methods. It was viewed as offering clear benefits in speeding up processes such as the drafting of documents, but this increased speed was also felt by some to have a negative impact in terms of increased client expectations and greater work pressure. Some respondents experienced difficulty in keeping email traffic to a manageable level and even took steps to limit use by clients.

Policies on email and Internet use within firms were common but these varied widely in their nature, the degree of formality involved, and the measures taken to enforce them. These policies were created in response to fears of legal liability or damage to the firm due to improper or malicious use of email, breaches of confidentiality, loss of control of documents after being sent, and inappropriate use of the Internet.

The introduction of ICT has raised issues associated with staff reluctance to embrace new technologies and the need for training to encourage staff to make greater use of ICT and overcome traditional mindsets.

Plans to expand the use of and access to email and the Internet by staff were driven by the needs of staff and clients, the working practices of other organisations and the further development of e-conveyancing. Access to broadband was a particular goal for some of those currently without it.

Web sites

Web sites tended to be used as an electronic brochure and firms had mixed opinions about their effectiveness in generating significant volumes of new business, or business that was a good 'fit' for the firm. As a result, web sites may not have been seen as a high priority in terms of the time and resource committed to it.

There was, however, some interest in investigating the introduction of interactive functions, such as online case management and legal databases containing points of law or precedents. On the other hand, there were fears that the use of web sites for completion of forms online may lead to an increased margin for error or to loss of fees.

Web sites could be of potential interest to firms currently without them but firms were often unconvinced that the benefits of web sites over traditional marketing methods were sufficient to justify the time and cost involved in setting up and maintaining a site.

Barriers to increased use of ICT

Whilst many were aware that the relative costs of ICT have come down over the years, cost remained a significant barrier to further use of ICT, not only the cost of initial investment in hardware and software but also the ongoing costs of maintenance and support, updates and staff training. The cost of expanding a firm's ICT capabilities can represent a significant proportion of a firm's fee income and may require the drive and commitment of an ICT 'champion' within the firm to establish the business case.

Security concerns appeared to be less of a constraint on investment in ICT. Firms were aware of the need for data security, though knowledge of specific security mechanisms, such as firewalls and password protection varied. However, there tended to be something of a fatalistic attitude towards data security, with a belief that systems can never be 100% secure, and some firms prefered to rely on 'good practice' among staff (such as not opening suspect emails) rather than to invest in physical security measures, that were perceived to be costly.

Other barriers to further use of ICT were: concerns about the reliability of systems; lack of adequate back-up facilities and the cost of introducing these; the need for training to encourage staff to use ICT and the cost of such training; the lack of time to plan for expansion, and problems integrating with existing systems.

How can the Law Society help?

A major concern about the information provided by the Law Society, such as the *Software Solutions Guide*, is that it adopts a 'one size fits all' approach, rather than tailored guidance and recommendation to firms of different sizes and types.

Firms are interested in receiving more support and guidance from the Law Society about relevant ICT issues. This could take the form of:

- guidelines or 'good practice' standards for issues such as security;
- lists of approved ICT consultants or suppliers;
- courses or seminars on ICT issues; and
- more frequent contact with law firms, either regularly, through an account manager or liaison officer, or on an ad hoc basis.

Whatever support is given, it is stressed that this should be targeted to the particular needs of smaller law firms and regionally.

Summary of conclusions

A striking feature of the focus groups was the range of experiences and behaviours represented in them, and the ad hoc approach to ICT development that characterised many firms. With some exceptions, change was often driven more by individual enthusiasm and commitment rather than by external market pressure.

Conversely, there were firms, and individuals within those firms, which took the, perhaps short-term, view that they were fairly comfortable with where they were in terms of ICT development. Age appeared to be a significant factor, with older staff tending to be less willing to adopt new working practices.

For those who were seeking to develop, the main difficulty lay in identifying and implementing a cost-effective ICT solution. The lack of an in-house specialist ICT function, in many cases, meant that firms depended upon external support and guidance. This was an area in which firms expressed the desire for Law Society involvement in providing direction and a central information resource.

Introduction

This report describes the findings from a qualitative research survey, conducted in June 2003, amongst small to medium-sized private practice firms (defined as those with ten or fewer partners) in England and Wales.

The research forms the second phase of a two-stage project designed to aid the Law Society's Practice Development Team in the development of a strategic policy to support small and medium-sized firms in their use of information and communication technology (ICT) and e-business. A major role of the Practice Development Team is to extend the markets for solicitors' services. A fundamental aspect of this function is to promote the uptake of ICT within the industry and to take appropriate action to assist in the development of legal e-business and enhance existing working practices.

The project concerned law firms' use of ICT and explored the barriers that may be hindering the further development and use of ICT for legal applications. The study was undertaken in order to identify ways in which the Law Society can realistically support and facilitate law firms in adapting to the rapidly changing legal services environment, with specific reference to ICT.

The study aimed to examine:

- solicitors' attitudes to ICT — from simple email to development of interactive web sites;
- solicitors' understanding of the short-term and long-term issues involved;
- practical and attitudinal barriers to using and developing ICT and electronic services; and
- opportunities for, and potential of, adapting legal services using ICT.

A total of 25 legal practices participated in eight discussion groups, each containing between two and five participants, conducted in London, Bristol, Birmingham and Manchester. The original intention was that there would be six to eight participants in each group but, although six to ten participants were recruited for each group, a substantial number failed to attend. The reasons for this have not been positively identified but the wide geographical area from which participants were recruited, because of the limited number of eligible firms within easy travelling distance of the discussion group venue, may have been a contributory factor.

It should be stressed, however, that 'mini-groups' of three to five respondents are common practice within the market research industry. They are regarded as particularly valuable for exploring a large number of complex topics in detail, as was the case in this research project, though the variety of opinions expressed may not be as great as in 'traditional' focus groups of six to eight participants.

It should also be stressed that, as qualitative research, the findings described in this report should not be taken as a measure of the extent to which such views are held amongst the wider population of law firms. Rather, it provides a detailed insight into issues, rationales and influences which serves to enrich understanding.

Participants were the individuals in their firms with most responsibility for ICT implementation. As noted elsewhere in this report, such individuals are often of crucial importance in driving forward the development of ICT within their firms, through their individual enthusiasm and commitment. It is therefore likely that the level of IT literacy shown by the respondents, as individuals, is exceptionally high, though this does not necessarily imply that their firms are untypical of the legal profession as a whole.

Law firms from two different size-bands were selected: four groups were conducted among firms with 1–3 partners and four with firms containing 3–10 partners. Both sizes of firm were also segmented by their level of ICT uptake (as indicated by whether they had a web site or not).

Before the focus groups were conducted, a pilot stage of four individual depth interviews was carried out, primarily to test the topic guide and to provide the basis for any recommended changes ahead of the main stage.

The respondents were obtained from those who had agreed to be contacted for a further study during the first phase of this project, and from the Law Society's REGIS database.

Section 1   The ICT environment

How PCs are being used

The focus group respondents reflected the pattern found in the earlier telephone survey in that use of PCs was found in all firms (96% in the telephone survey) but varied considerably in terms of the number or proportion of partners and staff using a PC and the sophistication of the systems and applications in use. Generally, respondents in the groups representing the larger law firms (consisting of between three and ten partners) had networked their PCs, whilst a few of the smaller law firms were using stand-alone PCs.

As in the telephone survey, the extent to which partners themselves used PCs appeared to be a function of individual preference and experience rather than a function of the size of the firm. Across both size groups there were examples of partners and fee-earners preferring to work traditionally, using dictation and secretarial support. In most firms, partners and fee-earners appeared to be free to choose how much they used computers personally, rather than being encouraged to follow a strict policy.

The most widely used PC applications were accounting/financial management packages and general office software (*eg* word processing and spreadsheets). Email usage and Internet access were less commonplace and some of the firms, particularly among the 1–3 partners group, made no use of either. The use of specialist legal applications, other than legal accounting software, was fairly uncommon and was mainly confined to firms in the larger size band. There was a perception, for example, that case management systems have been developed with large practices in mind and that they lack the flexibility that small firms require:

> *The larger systems are built so that you've got to do all the stages in order. You can't override it without supervisor authority.*
> 1–3 partners, with web site

Amongst firms using local area networks (LANs) , a common working practice regarding network access was for the senior partner or firm's administrator to establish specific permissions for each individual working within the firm. Network access would primarily be set up according to the role of each member of staff; a prime example of this would be specific permissions being set up for accounting staff:

> *Everyone has different permissions depending upon their role, people who do the bills they're obviously allowed into the accounts, there's no need for secretaries or anyone else to be in there.*
> 1–3 partners, without web site

> *Everybody has access to view the accounts but purely on a time recording basis, not on a billing basis.*
> 1–3 partners, with web site

Issues arose with regard to confidentiality and access to sensitive documentation that firms feel a need to be addressed. Some achieved this by having a mix of stand-alone computers as well as networked systems; one firm even went as far as word processing documents, printing them then deleting them from their hard drive.

As the telephone survey indicated, whereas use of word processing software was close to being universal (even among sole practitioner firms, 82% used it), the use of case management systems increased sharply with size of firm. Only a minority of firms with fewer than five partners had case management software, whereas 62% of firms with five to ten partners used it.

The qualitative study, in terms of access to case management or document management systems, found two prevailing issues. Some firms made their case or document management system available to everyone within the firm. Other firms provided all, or virtually all, of their fee-earners with full access, while other, non fee-earning members of the firm had restrictions on what they were allowed to view. This use of restrictions was more evident in larger firms, with more formal staff structures. Firms which had not placed access restrictions on either of these systems did admit that this was an area that they may explore in the near future, as the use of electronic communication grows. It was ever more important as the size of firm increased and issues around the supervision of junior staff arose.

Some firms that were using case management systems believed that they were not utilising the application to its full potential, because of difficulties in getting staff, particularly older staff, to change their working practices or difficulties in connecting it to other software used, such as accounts packages. In some cases, however, the use of case management systems had resulted in significant cost savings and even in firms being able to dispense with secretarial staff:

> I felt that the right case management package at the right price would be hugely beneficial for a smaller firm, because it is incredibly useful for cutting down and reducing administration overheads.
>
> 1–3 partners, with web site

Interestingly, on occasions where solicitors had experienced previous use of case management systems and had since moved to firms that did not work in this manner they found it something of a culture shock:

> I came out of the city into the suburbs for an easy life, and they didn't have a case management system and it was quite a big culture shock... If you don't have one I don't think you'd miss it but if you're used to having it, I missed it terribly.
>
> 1–3 partners, with web site

The issue of compatibility of software was raised by firms which had experienced problems when trying to maintain two separate packages working in tandem. Several respondents referred to compatibility problems when trying to get their accounting software to 'talk to' their case management systems, for example:

> The original thinking was that we bought two packages, case management and an accounts package from the same firm and that both would be developed together...we were sold down the river because now the two packages don't really talk to each other and aren't developed together anymore.
>
> 3–10 partners, without web site

> They acquired a financial package which we looked at but it simply wasn't developed enough and there wasn't enough support behind it, and the case management system for the financial package wasn't developed in the end as we wanted so we were stuck with two systems that weren't talking.
>
> 3–10 partners, without web site

Other compatibility issues related to calendar software and its utilisation in conjunction with other applications.

How the Internet is being used

The telephone survey indicated that whilst over 90% of firms with 10 or fewer partners had Internet access, the level of staff accessibility to it varies. The survey also established that access to the Internet by some or all partners was more common among larger firms (89% among firms with 5–10 partners) than among smaller ones (72% among firms with 2–4 partners and 54% among sole practitioners). The qualitative research suggested that where the benefits of the Internet were appreciated, and particularly where firms had been able to invest in training, access to the Internet was made more widely available. The benefits cited mainly concerned time and cost savings in research and in administrative tasks, such as the downloading of forms:

> *I suddenly saw the advantages of the Internet. I am now fully functional, I can operate without a secretary.*
> 3–10 partners, without web site

> *We find it very useful for our research, it's a time saving device.*
> 1–3 partners, with web site

These cost savings become especially apparent when broadband access to the Internet is available:

> *Since we've switched to broadband we've just saved so much money you know, I mean we're saving a lot more money on the telephone side of things than when just two of us were using it. So the broadband is really working.*
> 1–3 partners, with web site

However, in smaller firms, universal access did not necessarily lead to universal use:

> *Everybody in our firm can use the Internet, totally unlimited. But the vast majority of staff are older and it's hard work getting them to use a computer let alone getting them to use the Internet.*
> 1–3 partners, with web site

Other firms restricted the number of people that had Internet access from their desk by deliberate policy, fearing escalating costs, time-wasting or inappropriate usage. Sometimes, however, particularly in smaller, non-networked firms, Internet access was confined to one or two PCs because they were not connected to broadband and there were not enough telephone lines available to provide for all PC users.

However, among those using the Internet, it was generally regarded as a valuable resource. The web was used for a variety of different purposes, but mainly for legal information and research, obtaining legal forms and for conveyancing purposes by those who undertook such work. On some occasions, the Internet was used simply for general information, such as contact or location details for particular organisations.

Research and information gathering was mentioned by the majority of respondents who used the Internet. As well as being a source of reference material, the Internet had the advantage of immediacy. Particular mentions included:

- information on new precedents and acts of Parliament, rights and statutes;
- downloading the latest versions of litigation procedures and rules;
- government policy publications;
- instant transcriptions of tribunals and public meetings; and
- pilot schemes showing progress of court cases.

Some were overwhelmed by the information available on the Internet and the problems of locating relevant information. For these, portal sites and sites that provide links to others (the Society for Computers and Law was mentioned as an example) were considered to be helpful but were often seen as hit or miss:

> It's just a question of is it worth it, and you spend an hour or so searching around and you know that in a book you can look it up in five minutes but its free, there's no charge for it and it's usually very good.
> 1–3 partners, without web site

Online forms were starting to have an impact on working practices. The ability to download forms meant that firms had access to the latest versions, whereas previously some had unwittingly used out of date forms. Form downloads were also seen as labour and cost saving:

> Online access is far more attractive because it is available to everybody... It's always constantly up to date.

E-conveyancing

The topic of e-conveyancing was fairly controversial and surfaced on several occasions across the groups. Views on this topic varied considerably with several advantages and disadvantages being cited.

Most respondents were aware of the recent changes in the area of e-conveyancing, including one respondent who had taken part in a pilot scheme in Bristol, but some vagueness as to the current state of implementation and the timescales involved in further development was apparent, with some feeling that e-conveyancing represents a future 'ambition' rather than current practice:

> Conveyancing is going to be completely different in five years' time.
> 1–3 partners, without web site

A degree of scepticism was aired by a handful of respondents, believing that the recent developments in e-conveyancing seemed to benefit the Land Registry rather than the conveyancing professional. One such partner felt that the Land Registry was trying to increase its control over the whole process and admitted that their firm would wait and see how the system performed before going ahead and using it:

> I think it's important that solicitors try and take more control over the change that is happening. At the moment we're just being told what's happening and we're not doing much about it.
> 1–3 partners, with web site

The perception of a lack of sufficient consultation and input from law firms was a factor that worried a few respondents. There was a belief that although firms were informed of the recent changes regarding e-conveyancing, they had had little or no chance to air their views. One firm felt very strongly that conveyancing is an area of work where the quality of work might suffer with the widespread use of electronic communication:

> I am absolutely horrified that the Law Society and solicitors in general who work in this area aren't up in arms, this isn't a process that you can actually take away from the lawyer and still have the same end product... I've had two cases in the last year where the client came to me with a property other than the one that they'd bought!"
> 1–3 partners, with web site

Particular benefits that were cited in relation to e-conveyancing mainly centred around the benefits of using a system which would speed up the process considerably, reduce anxiety, enable electronic documentation and create the ability to transfer funds electronically.

One firm referred to a recent article in which the Land Registry had openly admitted that, at the moment, the system is not completely secure:

> They can't provide a secure basis for the Land Registry records.
> 1–3 partners, with web site

However, the same article was said to go on to state that the Land Registry was 'absolutely certain' that a secure system could be provided by the time the system was fully implemented, in three years' time.

How email is used

Consideration of the use of email must take into account communication with other legal service providers, with clients, and with other organisations.

Other legal service providers

Email correspondence with other solicitors or barristers is widespread — 86% of respondents to the telephone survey were in email communication with solicitors with other firms. According to a participant in the focus groups, email has particularly facilitated overseas work, especially where there were deadlines and time differences involved:

> I had a matrimonial case that was being litigated in Australia and without the e-mail facility it would have been impossible to deal with in the time constraints.
> 3–10 partners, without web site

The telephone survey indicated that the vast majority of firms used email in communication with clients, 93% used it for private clients, 88% for commercial clients, but gave no insight regarding the frequency with which it was used. The focus groups revealed that levels of email communication with clients differs sharply across law firms, largely according to the type of work that was being conducted and the type of client. Firms that conducted a large amount of legal aid work suggested that legal aid clients were less likely to own a PC and did not foresee that email would have a great impact on their communications with clients. However, as one respondent pointed out, there would be nothing to stop clients who did not have home PC access from using email at their local Internet café, if they were so predisposed. By contrast, in firms with a strong commercial client base and those where the majority of private client business was with those who could be described as 'young professionals', email correspondence was becoming much more commonplace and increasingly such clients nearly always expected to communicate in this way.

The advent of email raised issues relating to service expectations by clients. Some respondents felt that clients expected an instantaneous response to emails and that law firms ran the risk of being inundated with client demands. Whereas the use of email in commercial work was virtually unavoidable, a small 'high street' law firm may prefer not to offer the service openly to its private clients:

> *Inevitably most clients believe that they are the only client that you've got. You have got to give the best service you can but it becomes a nightmare if you are expected to respond within five minutes of every communication you get. You get some clients who are in such a state of mental anguish that they will send you five emails a day.*
> 3–10 partners, without web site

A few respondents mentioned that they would only declare the fact that they had an email facility if the client specifically asked for it, in order to keep email traffic at a more manageable level.

Other organisations

Firms communicating by email with other organisations, did not appear to be common practice amongst the participants. With regard to the courts, day-to-day correspondence was stated to be still undertaken largely by letter, with very little email communication coming from the courts. This lack of email communication with the courts had the potential to be highly frustrating:

> *Both ends have access to a considerable amount of technology but it has to convert into analogue in the middle and then has to be put back in.*
> 3–10 partners, without web site

However, there was some awareness of the Crown Courts' running of pilot schemes enabling case progress reports to be accessed online.

Electronic communication with the prison service was regarded as virtually non-existent, with a lack of adequate infrastructure making even more basic methods of communication, such as the telephone, problematic:

> *The Prison Service of course are even worse, telephone communication is difficult, moreover everything has to be faxed through; email just doesn't exist as a form of communication.*
> 3–10 partners, without web site

General implications

Although the extent to which email was being used seemed to be growing in many firms, most firms saw it as an additional and complementary method of communication rather than their main mode of communication. Most respondents were keen to say that email had not replaced other means of communication such as telephone or written mail, although several did highlight the fact that email usage had cut down on the number of telephone calls that they received. Two schools of thought seemed to emerge regarding the benefits and disadvantages of using email as a means of correspondence. Respondents appreciated the benefit of immediacy in using email, as well as its ability to speed up the process of revising draft documents. However, some expressed feelings that email is, in a sense, too quick — demanding immediate response. The downside of this is that greater email usage was thought to increase work pressure.

An additional consideration raised by one partner was that lack of ICT experience within a firm could mean that daily tasks actually took longer with the introduction of ICT:

> *If I was more computer literate I would certainly use email and Internet access a lot more, but I am very much a novice when it comes to computers and...everything probably takes five times longer than it should do.*
> 1–3 partners, without web site

A few respondents admitted to routinely printing out documentation after receiving it by email, in these cases most find it an easier way to work especially when required to review or make changes to documents.

Policies regarding use of Internet/email and how they were developed

Many firms had some Internet and email policy in place, although there was great variation in the strictness of policies and the rigour with which they are enforced. Some firms had polices for email and not for the Internet and vice versa. Policies included:

- formal written documents which employees have to sign, often strictly defining what can and cannot be sent by email or the purposes for which the Internet can be used;
- restriction of access to certain members of staff;
- less formal guidelines based on common sense and trust (including allowing personal use of the Internet outside working hours); and
- the use of email disclaimers.

On the whole, firms, that conducted a large amount of commercial work, felt that a more formal policy provided greater protection, as this is an area in which email use was more prevalent (as indicated earlier). In addition, commercial organisations were felt to be more likely to take action against law firms, in the event of misuse of email.

The use of formal policies, such as email disclaimers, were in response to fears of:

- Liability and risk management

> *We're currently researching software packages that will scan documents in order to see what exactly junior members are sending out. They are actually sending an advice letter to a client that contains information that hasn't been checked by a partner. There is software that can scan and look for these high risk words like 'we promise'.*
> 1–3 partners, with web site

- Confidentiality

> *Disclaimers are more on the basis that this is confidential information and if you got hold of it, watch out, don't use it.*
> 3–10 partners, without web site

- Control of documents after they are sent

Only recently it's been drummed into me is how an email is virtually a public document once you send it. People can open it, read it, change it and then put it back again and it's not a secure document.
3–10 partners, with web site

- Damage to firm due to malicious emails
One solicitor had heard about another firm's problems:

Some disgruntled employee sent out an email to a load of people saying 'X were a load of shysters' and X have got hold of this communication and were able to take action against the company that sent it.
3–10 partners, without web site

- Inappropriate use of the Internet

Kind of worried about how much time they're going to spend on it playing games or doing whatever they're doing.
1–3 partners, with web site

In some firms, senior staff or line managers actively monitored Internet use, varying from monitoring all emails to checking a proportion of traffic:

Any external emails coming into an individual are copied by our email server to a partner responsible; so they see all the incoming e-mails and any outgoing emails are blind copied to a partner.
1–3 partners, with web site

Other firms felt that this kind of monitoring was unworkable or inappropriate, either because the volume of email/Internet use was too large or because of the firm's culture, which, in firms of this size, was often less formal and based more on trust:

Because everybody has access to the email at work, it's very difficult to impose, especially in a small firm when you feel that you have got a degree of rapport with your staff.
1–3 partners, with web site

Some firms, however, were looking into the use of specialised monitoring software to circumvent this etiquette barrier.

Where more formal policies were in place these had often been developed by senior partners — although one firm had based its policy on one used by a US accountancy firm that they found over the Internet. Other less formal policies seem to have evolved from day-to-day working and concentrated more on facilitating good working practice (*eg* if a partner was ill then their emails are forwarded on to a secretary).

Issues involved in introduction of ICT

Staff reluctance to embrace new technologies and training were the largest issues relating to the introduction of new ICT. Almost all participants could cite instances of 'Luddites' in their firms and some even admitted it of themselves. In most cases younger staff were more comfortable with new ICT than older staff. Even firms which had embraced ICT ran into problems of a generation gap relating to ICT use and non-use:

We made efforts to be computerised from an early stage, but new staff have come in, the younger ones are fully literate with email and computers generally, but the older staff who have come in from other firms, they've found it very difficult to change.
3–10 partners, without web site

As well as having to overcome often ingrained mindsets, almost all firms felt that more training was needed, but that time and access to training was often a stumbling block. One firm without a dedicated training resource had a partner take on this role:

It's finding the time to sit down with them and showing them what to do...because we've got lots and lots of work we need to do. It's difficult finding the time to show people what to do.
1–3 partners, with web site

Many firms believed that the Internet and email have changed working practices with clients. As mentioned before, in general, they were felt to have raised service expectations from clients. Whilst some firms had struggled to adapt, others felt that this was a positive thing:

Clients who have become more empowered will want a different form of service. They will want 24-hour offices. As the web becomes more important, there is a move towards having a portal that they can look at their case file, they can communicate and find out what's going on.
3–10 partners, without web site

The expansion of the Internet brings other problems. One partner had found difficulty navigating through the wealth of information on the web and felt that delegating such work to a central resource within the firm would be extremely beneficial in terms of saving fee-earning time. With increased access (or projected increased access) some partners felt that more stringent policies will have to be put into place.

Less obviously, things that had traditionally been seen as benefits of new ICT had sometimes brought unforeseen disadvantages. For example, the speed and cost benefits that accrue to clients through the use of ICT have created increased commercial pressures on law firms:

I think the end result of getting work done quicker is that we're expected to be paid much less for the work you are doing. So ultimately you have to do four times as much work to be paid what you have been paid for one before.
3–10 partners, without web site

Future plans

Many firms had plans to expand use and access to the Internet along with email for staff. This was driven by a number of factors.

- The needs of staff (*eg* access to information/electronic forms).

- The needs of clients:

It enables you to give the service to commercial clients that they really want because...most of my commercial clients don't like the way we traditionally deal with them.
1–3 partners, with web site

- The working practices of other firms and other organisations (*eg* courts, commercial companies, government *etc*):

It's coming, it's building, on routine conveyancing now, we're getting other firms who are writing to us by email.
1–3 partners, with web site

- The changes to conveyancing:

It's speeding up the process, being able to get searches back in such a short space of time, that's what clients want at the end of the day, so you provide a good service. And you want to get ahead, or you need to be equal.
1–3 partners, with web site

Some firms planned to extend the use of ICT beyond just email and Internet access so that more staff could work remotely, partly in response to client expectation but also in response to the cost of office space. One such firm had wanted a virtual private network but this was too expensive to implement at present. Broadband was a future intention for some firms currently without it, especially with the introduction of e-conveyancing. For smaller firms, particularly those without web sites, the problem they perceived was that their current volume of email and Internet usage did not justify the extra expense of broadband.

There was also evidence of firms using remote secretarial services via email, for example, creating and sending digital files of dictation to a service provider who returned typed documents by email. As well as increased quality in recording and the ability to work from home, this development has the potential to cut costs and staff further. One respondent, having previously sent voice files to a secretary in the provinces, was now sending them overseas:

Distance is no longer a relevance. We're using secretaries in Bangladesh, which varies between £3.50 a day at the most it's £2.57 an hour. The timescale works entirely in your favour because if you email in the evening it's there for you first thing in the morning.
3–10 partners, without web site

Other items of ICT which were mentioned as future plans included:

- electronic encryption; and
- electronic signatures.

Apart from the cost of investment, which can represent a significant proportion of a small firm's income, a major constraint on implementing these future plans was the sheer lack of time to plan and to prioritise such investment, particularly as most decision-makers in smaller firms were fee-earning partners, rather than dedicated ICT specialists. This lack of 'thinking time' can make it difficult to weigh up whether a particular investment in ICT is worthwhile, in terms of business benefits:

The real trouble is trying to think 'What problem can it solve for me now?'...It's got to save me time so I can go and make money or it's got to improve the service I give to the client.
3–10 partners, without web site

Section 2 Web sites

How firms use their web sites

The majority of firms in the survey, 59% stated that they maintained purely brochure web sites. Only 20% maintained sites with some form of interactive function. The focus groups reflected the telephone survey findings. The main purpose of sites was to provide an introduction to the firm, its capabilities and contact details. Where respondents worked in firms with web sites, enthusiasm for the company web site varied. Some felt that it made a quick impact and was successful:

> I was conscious of wanting to make sure that even though I'm a small firm, I might sometimes be higher up the list...I do know some business is coming in through the web site.
>
> 1–3 partners, with web site

However, others took a more cautious view of the web site's ability to generate business. One respondent felt that their site was quite basic and that insufficient time and resource had been invested to make the site effective as an advertising medium. One particular issue was the design of the site so that it ranks near the top of the list when using search engines:

> The web site is one thing but getting people to be attracted to it, by whatever means there happen to be, is apparently a very strange world.
>
> 3–10 partners with web site

In addition, the enquiries that a web site generated were not always thought to be appropriate to the firm's business. One firm, which had previously used a web site, had since discontinued it:

> You can spend all day long answering enquiries from people from well outside your catchment area, who would have no interest in instructing you.
>
> 3–10 partners, without web site

Funding for web sites could sometimes therefore be a fairly low priority, where firms preferred a more traditional approach to marketing and business generation:

> Ours is just another client contacting way, and that's what clients will do if they're comfortable. I like to retain the personal touch.
>
> 1–3 partners, with web site

Nevertheless, some innovative marketing approaches were being used. One respondent had introduced a system whereby email addresses were collected from web site 'hits' and the firm's newsletter was automatically emailed back to them.

Use of/interest in interactive functions on web sites

A number of the firms participating in the focus groups had web sites with a degree of interactivity on them, whilst others were keen to investigate the potential benefits of certain functions. The interactive functions prompted for discussion were:

- Online case management, which would be accessible to clients. This generated the most positive response with some companies already having implemented it or wanting to. The main concern for all (both those with this function and those interested in it) was security. This had two main aspects: (1) ensuring through password protection that only the correct client has access to their files:

They've got to give certain details and a password and only if those things check are they then allowed to that part of our computer network which contains their files and no-one else's...as a double check, the passwords are changed every couple of months.
3–10 partners with web site

  and (2) that the case management file shown on screen was a read-only 'mirror image' containing information that had been uploaded by the law firm itself and could not be tampered with by the client:

I don't want anybody being able to come in and change a document without my approval.
1–3 partners with web site

- Legal databases (containing points of law, precedents etc.): Just one firm had this facility although another was developing it. Others were not in favour of this for a number of reasons. Some felt they would effectively be giving out advice over the Internet for free, others felt that without proper expert opinion, this information could be misinterpreted. Also, the time and financial investment needed to keep such a database up to date was thought not to be justified:

We're actually feeding legal advice over the net, it might not actually be paying us any money at the moment, but from a time point of view the trainees currently spend far longer having an interaction with the client online than they do trying to get the client come in and pay £40 for an interview.
1–3 partners with web site

- Use of online documents and form filling. This caused opinion to be polarised. Some felt that this function could save time and reduce workloads. Others believed that clients should be present in the office when completing paperwork, otherwise the margin for error could be increased. Additionally, many respondents thought that clients would be less inclined to pay for a service, if they had to fill in their own forms. The latter view suggests that there is concern within the profession that increased use of ICT devalues the work of solicitors.

Other interactive offerings mentioned spontaneously as being in use by some firms included:

- E-marketing where a pop-up window collected email addresses of people signing up for newsletters.

- Interactive Q&A section. One respondent referred to a member of a sole practitioners' group to which he belonged having set up an interactive site relating to Tenant Law, which was beginning to generate some business. One issue regarding this function mirrored that of legal databases, that is, simply giving legal advice over the Internet for free. Another was that dealing with the relatively simple types of issue covered by such Q&A approaches (eg statutory driving offences), could be appropriately handled by trainees through personal interaction with clients, giving them experience.

- Online conveyancing forms. These can involve such things as a seller's list of fixtures and fittings. However, the respondent who referred to this was anxious to emphasise that such online form-filling would be inappropriate for the drafting of legal documents.

Reasons for not setting up a web site

A number of the firms without web sites had at some point considered (or would consider) setting up a web site. The initial expectations were that a web site's main purpose would be to generate business. The main barriers to setting up a web site are:

- Cost; mentioned by most firms as the biggest barrier, which some believed would not be justified by the returns in terms of additional business

- The time taken to set up and maintain a site. One partner had even been on a web site course but had yet to find time to put it into practice:

You've got to spend a lot of time making it interesting and up to date otherwise it's dead in the water.
1–3 partners, without web site

- The perception that web sites were not useful to small firms — held particularly by the 'High Street' lawyer who felt comfortable with the level and type of business generated by traditional marketing methods (eg the Yellow Pages, personal recommendation and a visible local presence) and believed that a web site would not help to generate any more business of a type that the firm would be interested in handling:

Perhaps a web site may attract the wrong sort of people anyway.
1–3 partners, without web site

Some firms expressed interest in some of the secure interactive functions used on the web sites of larger firms but were not sure that these would work for smaller firms.

- The perception that web sites are most applicable to firms with specialist disciplines, that are hard for potential clients to identify from general listings of solicitors:

I did consider having a web page because I was a notary, not because I was a solicitor...because I know that people do go on the web and click on 'notary'.
1–3 partners, without web site

- The lack of expertise to maintain the site. One firm did not want to keep having to go to a third party every time it was necessary to change the content of the site.

Despite these barriers, several focus group participants were considering setting up web sites in the future. (In the telephone survey, roughly a third of firms currently without a web site claimed to be planning to have one within the next twelve months.) The discussions revealed that this was often because firms perceived that working practices within the profession as a whole were moving in that direction, and it was unclear in some cases, whether there were any positive 'drivers' towards introduction of a web site other than a desire to go with the tide.

One partner predicted that it will become necessary to introduce a web site in the foreseeable future:

> *It will probably be a Law Society requirement or a Legal Service Commission. You are now required to have all this stuff in their books which are electronic so the next stage is you have to have a web site.*
>
> 3–10 partners, without web site

Section 3   **Barriers to increased use of ICT**

Cost/financial investment

The issue most at the forefront of respondents' minds as a barrier to the increasing use of ICT was cost. Although some appreciated that relative costs had come down and others had successfully managed to apply for grants, that was viewed as a major barrier not only for initial outlay but for ongoing expenses such as maintenance, updating software, hardware, virus checkers etc. and other facilities. Not all of these were affordable to some and therefore sacrifices had to be made:

> *When you're working on the tightest overheads that you possibly can work on, some things have to be left.*
> 1–3 partners, with web site

Respondents cited many different types of cost that were associated with the implementation of ICT:

- Hardware — one firm bought a new system which cost £60,000, which represented a quarter of the firm's turnover for the previous year. Another had engaged in a long-term programme to transform the firm's ICT capabilities:

> *We went from two, three computers to now, 30 staff, 30 computers, we've got two ADSL fixed lines, we've got a main server, we invested £250,000 which we've spread over five years, but that again I would say is about 30% a year for the next five years if we survive that long.*
> 1–3 partners, with web site

As the quotation illustrates, such investment requires a good deal of personal commitment and, indeed, courage to proceed with.

- Software — firms which used off-the-shelf specialist software often considered the costs of such software, and of the licences and updates, too high:

> *I had the Encyclopaedia of Forms and Precedents in book form and Butterworth's offered it to me on disc and online. It sounded perfect and it was £1,500 for that, but there were ever spiralling re-licence fees...updates, constant updates, £400 for this, £400 for that, and the bills mount up to the extent that I had to say, sorry, we cannot do this any more.*
> 3–10 partners, without web site

One firm was charged £5 every time they accessed a form, another spent £12,000 on licensing costs in a year. A lack of competition amongst specialist software firms was blamed for these perceived high costs. Firms which had experienced compatibility problems were generally reluctant to start from scratch after years of continual investment with their current software/systems:

> *You have such an investment over the years, you can't afford to let it all go and spend another £100/£200,000 on another package and start from scratch.*
> 3–10 partners, without web site

Some firms opted for tailor-made software; one paid £12,000 for a program:

> *£12,000 seems like a lot of money when you say to somebody 'I'm going to write you a case management system specifically for your practice that will require me being here every day for three months to see every aspect of your practice so that I can integrate what you want'.*
> 1–3 partners, with web site

In this instance, the investment was thought to be a worthwhile and cost-effective solution but, again, convincing other members of the firm of this had depended on the personal drive and commitment of the individual to establish the business case.

- Consultancy and support fees — smaller firms generally lacked an ICT specialist in-house and relied on external contractors for day-to-day support, advice on upgrades and so on. Cost in such circumstances was a constraint on the level of relationship that was formed with such contractors:

> *I wouldn't want to pay a contract. I mean (the sub-contractor) has offered a contract but it's very expensive. You know you have to have a regular payment so that in theory you can just pick up a phone and get somebody there within 24 hours or less but you know that is quite expensive.*
> 3–10 partners, with web site

- Training — staff training in how to use new software was deemed to be essential in order to encourage staff to want to use ICT but it represented an additional cost. One respondent referred to grants that are available for such training, for example in Development Areas or through local Chambers of Commerce but others were unaware of these.

One specific concern among firms involved with legal aid was associated with the franchise requirements for legal aid, which were thought to be very much based upon computerised accounting and time recording:

> *The Legal Services Commission is changing constantly the requirements, so again, (they) have got to come in, have got to give you two days training on how to do this and that, £500 a day.*
> 3–10 partners, without web site

- Costs associated with virus checking, security and back-up, which were sometimes seen as a last priority in terms of IT budget:

> *We have had no back-up and no maintenance support for two and a half years on the system.*
> 1–3 partners, with web site

Confidentiality and security

In general, firms (regardless of size) felt that no matter what they do, their systems would never be 100% safe from external threat:

> *We're going to be vulnerable to people who have skills and resources far greater than anything we could ever afford.*
> 3–10 partners, without web site

> *If Microsoft gets hacked on a regular basis, I don't think I'm going to be able to stop anybody.*
> 1–3 partners, without web site

Although something of a fatalistic attitude towards security was apparent in these quotes, as the same can be said about attitudes to security of paper files — a number of respondents cited experiences of risks such as burglary, fire or loss of files — security cannot be said to be a major constraint on investment in ICT.

All firms were aware of the need for security in order to maintain confidentiality of the client and to conform to The Data Protection Act. However, firms' concerns appeared to centre mainly around establishing good office procedures, encouraging staff to treat electronic communication as confidential documents in the same way as normal post:

> *It's strange how everybody looks at (email) and thinks it doesn't exist, it's not real unless it churns out a piece of paper. So we've got policies on that.*
> 3–10 partners, without web site

Knowledge of security mechanisms varies. The use of password protection was frequently mentioned, although some of the smaller firms did not feel that it was necessary because they trusted all of their staff not to abuse access. Some larger firms limited access to parts of their system to certain members of staff. Some thus found it hard to balance a need for confidentiality and the need for a workable system:

> *Sometimes people have access to parts of the system that you wouldn't necessarily want to, but you have to balance it. You can't tie everything down so tightly that you need to employ three people just to administer what people can and can't do.*
> 3–10 partners, with web site

Firms with networks and those using Intranets were aware of external threats of unauthorised access and hacking and usually had firewalls and additional measures in place for dealing with these. One firm had been the victim of a hacker who had managed to obtain the password of a partner. Just one firm claimed to be unconcerned by the threat of hackers because they had judged that, as a small firm with purely local concerns, they were not a 'prime target' and that there was nothing on their system that they are worried about others seeing. By contrast, another firm went as far as word processing documents, printing the file then deleting the electronic version. Many firms were also aware of viruses and the potential damage that can be done by them, but for some there were problems implementing virus screeners. One firm that installed a screening program found that it crashed their system. Others did not have the money to implement such precautions and relied on staff vigilance.

The cost of security was an issue. Some firms (particularly smaller firms) relied on third parties for the provision of security, which others could afford. Even one larger firm, which had in-house IT support, sometimes struggled to find money for staff to oversee security. Some firms rely on staff taking measures (*eg* not opening email from unknown sources), rather than physical security measures, but even in these cases it was felt that there can be costs involved through the provision of further staff training in this area:

> *Not all the machines are as secure as they could be. We need staff training and let staff know what to look out for.*
> 3–10 partners, with web site

Reliability and back-up

Some firms felt that the unreliability of their systems was hindering progress. One partner, for example, complained that their system was always crashing so that expansion is not felt to be an option. For smaller firms, particularly those without web sites, reliability and fear of their files being deleted (either through system crashes or by human error) had led them away from the paperless office as they felt they needed a hard copy:

> *I think you want to see something physical there and the thought of it all disappearing in one click of a button is...*
> 3–10 partners, without web site

Firms were mostly aware of data back-up systems but actual use varied. Larger firms and those with web sites, tended to have better back up systems, these ranged from off-site back up servers, to discs or tapes being taken offsite or kept in fireproof safes overnight. Some smaller firms, however, appeared to backup data very rarely or not at all. Although some of the firms without back-up systems were investigating means of back-up, the main barrier again here is perceived to be cost.

Training

Two main issues were raised relating to training on a new system. Firstly, there was the belief that firms would not get the full benefit from any new ICT application unless training was provided:

> *If the software or hardware is not introduced in a way that people can grasp straight away and you haven't got the time to simply see it through, it falls into disuse.*
> 3–10 partners, without web site

Secondly, however, there was also a concern about the staff time that is taken for training — the time taken out of their working day to receive or administer training is lost fee-earning time. In some cases, there was no specialist trainer and it fell to individuals (sometimes fee-earners) in the company to find the time to train other members of staff:

> *It's finding the time to sit down with them and showing them what to do, because we've all got lots and lots of work we need to do.*
> 1–3 partners, with web site

Other barriers

Other barriers to increased take up/expansion of ICT include:

- Lack of planning time; some feel that they do not have sufficient time to decide on their exact requirements for a system and then to implement them:

  It's a very substantial amount of thinking time applied to plan ahead for strategic change.
  3–10 partners, without web site

- Problems integrating with existing systems.

Section 4   The Law Society

Awareness of/attitudes to what Law Society provides

Most of the focus group respondents were aware of information provided by the Law Society. However, some felt that there was too much information, which they do not have time to read and digest, whilst others feel that the information provided is unsatisfactory:

> *My only dealings with the Law Society have been generally unsatisfactory when I asked them for some information, which has never been forthcoming.*
> 3–10 partners, without web site

Some of the information provided, for example in articles in the Gazette, was felt to be geared largely towards larger firms and advanced users or ICT specialists:

> *They're talking about management software and, (for) people who have only just bought their computer, that's pretty academic...they'll say that still only 50% of fee-earners have got a computer on their desk and then in the same breath they'll start a huge article on some very specialised IT topic.*
> 3–10 partners, with web site

It is also felt the Law Society has a 'one size fits all' approach to ICT that is not relevant to them:

> *I've come across publications that are sent out. It's ten pages long and it is supposed to cover every firm in the land. The security implications of Slaughter and May are rather different to [a one man band].*
> 3–10 partners, without web site

Opinion regarding the Law Society's *Software Solutions Guide* were somewhat mixed. Awareness of the Guide was high and it was found by some to be extremely useful and comprehensive:

> *They send us something every year, all the case management and accounts packages.*
> 1–3 partners, with web site

> *I can visualise the Law Society's booklet with finance packages. They just went through 20 providers and gave them ticks and crosses and it's just really, really good.*
> 1–3 partners, without web site

However, some felt that the Guide was insufficiently reliable:

> *People rely on it to their detriment. It must be sufficiently authoritative, sufficiently accurate for somebody to be able to go out and purchase.*
> 1–3 partners, with web site

Others had been on courses and presentations provided by the Law Society. Here, although opinions of those who had attended these courses were generally positive, some felt that the Law Society could have made more specific recommendations in relation to appropriateness for firms of different sizes and types.

> *The difference in price between some of (the recommended software) says to me that it can't possibly be that they do the same thing.*
> 1–3 partners, with web site

One partner mentioned a telephone help-line from the Law Society, but that he did not use it because it was too expensive (calls are currently charged at local rates).

What more the Law Society should do

In general, firms wanted more support and specific guidance from the Law Society about relevant ICT issues. Needs varied with the size of the company, but most firms, regardless of size, looked to the Law Society for direction, but given the diversity and size of the profession the Law Society may not be in a position to give such specific advice:

> Shouldn't the Law Society be telling us what we want? We know we want something but we don't know what it is.
> 3–10 partners, without web site

Some want this in the form of guidelines or a set of standards for issues such as security:

> They've [Law Society] got the clout to hire the best computer people in the country, which we can't do. Collectively they could come up with guidance.
> 3–10 partners, with web site

Others desired lists of approved suppliers/consultants or felt that the Law Society should provide IT consultants at a discounted rate. Some expressed an interest in attending courses or seminars on IT security.

One respondent suggested the setting up of an account manager or liaison officer at the Law Society, as was available with the Legal Services Commission:

> So that you have a personal relationship with somebody from the Law Society, not as a means of a big stick to you, or dealing with complaints or anything like that but as a means of liaison...With the Legal Services Commission, you do have an Account Manager and, like it or not, that person will visit you and you have an audit every year or two years. I don't see that necessarily as an adverse thing, I find it a positive experience.
> 3–10 partners, with web site

However, others simply wanted more contact on an ad hoc basis:

> You just want to get confirmation that you're on the right track and just to meet up as well.
> 1–3 partners, with web site

For others, support and direction meant more but well targeted information. Smaller firms expressed the view that the Law Society did not show that they understood their particular needs and needed to provide information specifically tailored to the small legal practice. One partner wanted to see a dedicated web site for sole practitioners. Other firms want more links to relevant web sites and several firms suggested a monthly newsletter focusing on the latest issues. Others expressed the need for localised information:

> They need to remember that there are different regions and it shouldn't all be south-east concentrated because there's nothing that can turn people off more than to see a huge long list of 50 suppliers that are all down in the south-east and there's one in the north-west.
> 3–10 partners, with web site

> It's quite prejudicial but my view is that they are really geared to the large firms and they have very little interest in the small firms quite frankly.
> 1–3 partners, without web site

Conclusions

The firms covered by this study, *ie* those with ten or fewer partners, are largely characterised by an ad hoc approach to the use of ICT, determined more by the preferences of individual partners and fee-earners than by overriding market forces or drivers of change. Whilst all firms had PCs, the extent and manner of their use was generally a matter of personal choice rather than organisational policy. In this context, the age profile of firms was important, with younger staff being more ready to embrace new technology, whilst older staff lacked the experience, training (and sometimes the willingness) to adopt new working practices.

External pressures driving the development of ICT were apparent in the following ways:

- firms with a high proportion of commercial clients are obliged to use email more extensively, to meet client expectations of speed of response;
- firms specialising in legal aid work were under an exceptional degree of pressure to reduce overhead costs to remain profitable and some appear to view technology as a way to reduce the number of administrative staff relative to the number of fee-earners; and
- compared with other law firms, those specialising in personal injury tended to have large numbers of staff (working in claims departments) relative to the number of partners in the firm, and their state of technological development was more akin to that of larger firms, rather than the type of firm generally represented in this study.

Examples of firms oblivious to external drivers were also evident. This suggests that there are typical 'high street firms', serving a predominantly private client base, who feel none of these pressures and operate in a 'comfort zone' in which the firm is perfectly happy with its current type and volume of work and feeling little inclination to change working practices.

Use of PCs was often confined to the standard office software applications (word processing, spreadsheets) and accounting packages. The benefits of case management systems were widely appreciated but where such software had been introduced, this had sometimes given rise to problems of compatibility with existing accounts-based office systems. Equally, compatibility issues arose when trying to upgrade existing systems or add to them. This in turn led to another of the key issues identified in the research: the lack of, or difficulty in identifying, reliable sources of IT support. Widespread distrust of software suppliers themselves was very apparent.

Email use can best be described as reactive rather than proactive. If clients (particularly commercial clients) wished to correspond by email, solicitors were willing to follow suit — but the data indicated that they may not be inclined to initiate increased use of email because of the raising of client expectations, with regard to speed of response, that would follow.

Internet use for work purposes again seemed to be largely a matter of personal discretion. Whilst the benefits of the Internet were widely recognised, as a tool for research and for downloading current legal forms, respondents expressed the view that sites were often found only by chance. The lack of a central resource for identifying useful sites was felt to be a major drawback.

Most firms recognised the need for a policy, either formal or informal, on the use of email and the Internet. However, in the smallest firms, there is generally a feeling that there is sufficient internal rapport within the firm to ensure that there are no major problems.

Where firms had web sites, these were generally used for marketing purposes only. Client access to case management updates was felt to be a potentially useful feature, though not yet widely implemented. However, there were doubts about the usefulness of a firm's web site as a legal database (because of lack of time to keep the site up-to-date) or for interactive completion of forms (because of concerns about potential for error and for loss of revenue).

Any consideration of barriers to further uptake of ICT needs to be viewed in the context that many firms are fairly comfortable with the present state of affairs. There was often little evidence of 'push' from within firms to improve their capabilities, and the ICT industry was often viewed as offering solutions where there was no perceived problem to begin with. However, a number of barriers were identified including:

- the difficulty of implementing cost-effective ICT solutions;
- concerns over security (though the impossibility of achieving 100% security is largely accepted as a fact of life);
- reliability of systems; and
- lack of training and expertise.

All these areas are those in which external support and guidance would be appreciated and in which firms would like the Law Society to provide direction and a central information resource. This could involve:

- lists of approved software, suppliers and consultants;
- provision of training/guides to training resources;
- lists of/links to useful web sites; and
- guidelines on security issues.

However, a common concern was that the information and support currently provided by the Law Society is geared too much towards the need of larger firms and that further activity should be targeted more specifically, not only to smaller firms in general but also recognising the needs of particular niche areas, such as legal aid practices.

www.research.lawsociety.org.uk

Annual statistical reports
- *Trends in the solicitors' profession*

Fact sheet information series
- *Key facts on the solicitors' profession in England and Wales*
- *Distribution of firms, solicitors and turnover*
- *Number of Solicitors on the Roll and practising certificate holders since 1950*
- *Women solicitors*
- *Private practice solicitors' salaries*
- *Solicitors' working lives and clients*
- *Solicitors' use of and access to IT and the Internet*
- *Solicitors' firms*

Research study series: executive summaries

SRU publications list and order form

Research links

Strategic Research Unit

The Law Society
113 Chancery Lane
London WC2A 1PL

Enquiry Line: 020 7320 5623
Fax: 020 7316 5642

EnquiriesSRU@lawsociety.org.uk